# CREDIT CARD
# PAYMENT TRACKER

_____

_____

# DEDICATION

This Credit Card Payment Planner Book is dedicated to all the people out there who want to keep track and record credit card payments and document their findings in the process.

You are my inspiration for producing books and I'm honored to be a part of keeping all of your credit card payment notes and records organized.

This journal notebook will help you record the details of your payments.

Thoughtfully put together with these sections to record: Company, Amount Owed, Minimum Payment, Interest Rate, Due Date, Date, Starting Balance, Payment Value, and Remaining Balance.

# HOW TO USE THIS BOOK

The purpose of this book is to keep all of your Credit Card Payment notes all in one place. It will help keep you organized.

This Credit Card Payment Planner Book will allow you to accurately document every detail about your credit card payments.

Here are examples of the prompts for you to fill in and write about your experience in this book:

1. Company

2. Amount Owed

3. Minimum Payment

4. Interest Rate

5. Due Date

6. Date

7. Starting Balance

8. Payment Value

9. Remaining Balance

# CREDIT CARD PAYMENTS

**COMPANY**

**AMOUNT OWED**

**MINIMUM PAYMENT**

**INTEREST RATE**

**DUE DATE**

| DATE | STARTING BALANCE | PAYMENT VALUE | REMAINING BALANCE |
|------|------------------|---------------|-------------------|
|      |                  |               |                   |
|      |                  |               |                   |
|      |                  |               |                   |
|      |                  |               |                   |
|      |                  |               |                   |
|      |                  |               |                   |
|      |                  |               |                   |
|      |                  |               |                   |
|      |                  |               |                   |
|      |                  |               |                   |
|      |                  |               |                   |
|      |                  |               |                   |
|      |                  |               |                   |
|      |                  |               |                   |
|      |                  |               |                   |
|      |                  |               |                   |
|      |                  |               |                   |
|      |                  |               |                   |
|      |                  |               |                   |
|      |                  |               |                   |
|      |                  |               |                   |
|      |                  |               |                   |
|      |                  |               |                   |
|      |                  |               |                   |

# CREDIT CARD PAYMENTS

COMPANY

AMOUNT OWED

MINIMUM PAYMENT

INTEREST RATE

DUE DATE

| DATE | STARTING BALANCE | PAYMENT VALUE | REMAINING BALANCE |
|------|------------------|---------------|-------------------|
|      |                  |               |                   |
|      |                  |               |                   |
|      |                  |               |                   |
|      |                  |               |                   |
|      |                  |               |                   |
|      |                  |               |                   |
|      |                  |               |                   |
|      |                  |               |                   |
|      |                  |               |                   |
|      |                  |               |                   |
|      |                  |               |                   |
|      |                  |               |                   |
|      |                  |               |                   |
|      |                  |               |                   |
|      |                  |               |                   |
|      |                  |               |                   |
|      |                  |               |                   |
|      |                  |               |                   |
|      |                  |               |                   |
|      |                  |               |                   |
|      |                  |               |                   |
|      |                  |               |                   |
|      |                  |               |                   |
|      |                  |               |                   |

# CREDIT CARD PAYMENTS

**COMPANY**

**AMOUNT OWED**

**MINIMUM PAYMENT**

**INTEREST RATE**

**DUE DATE**

| DATE | STARTING BALANCE | PAYMENT VALUE | REMAINING BALANCE |
|------|------------------|---------------|-------------------|
|  |  |  |  |
|  |  |  |  |
|  |  |  |  |
|  |  |  |  |
|  |  |  |  |
|  |  |  |  |
|  |  |  |  |
|  |  |  |  |
|  |  |  |  |
|  |  |  |  |
|  |  |  |  |
|  |  |  |  |
|  |  |  |  |
|  |  |  |  |
|  |  |  |  |
|  |  |  |  |
|  |  |  |  |
|  |  |  |  |
|  |  |  |  |
|  |  |  |  |
|  |  |  |  |

# CREDIT CARD PAYMENTS

| COMPANY | |
|---|---|

| AMOUNT OWED | |
|---|---|

| MINIMUM PAYMENT | |
|---|---|

| INTEREST RATE | |
|---|---|

| DUE DATE | |
|---|---|

| DATE | STARTING BALANCE | PAYMENT VALUE | REMAINING BALANCE |
|---|---|---|---|
| | | | |
| | | | |
| | | | |
| | | | |
| | | | |
| | | | |
| | | | |
| | | | |
| | | | |
| | | | |
| | | | |
| | | | |
| | | | |
| | | | |
| | | | |
| | | | |
| | | | |
| | | | |
| | | | |
| | | | |
| | | | |
| | | | |
| | | | |
| | | | |
| | | | |

# CREDIT CARD PAYMENTS

**COMPANY** _____

**AMOUNT OWED** _____

**MINIMUM PAYMENT** _____

**INTEREST RATE** _____

**DUE DATE** _____

| DATE | STARTING BALANCE | PAYMENT VALUE | REMAINING BALANCE |
|------|------------------|---------------|-------------------|
|      |                  |               |                   |
|      |                  |               |                   |
|      |                  |               |                   |
|      |                  |               |                   |
|      |                  |               |                   |
|      |                  |               |                   |
|      |                  |               |                   |
|      |                  |               |                   |
|      |                  |               |                   |
|      |                  |               |                   |
|      |                  |               |                   |
|      |                  |               |                   |
|      |                  |               |                   |
|      |                  |               |                   |
|      |                  |               |                   |
|      |                  |               |                   |
|      |                  |               |                   |
|      |                  |               |                   |
|      |                  |               |                   |
|      |                  |               |                   |
|      |                  |               |                   |
|      |                  |               |                   |
|      |                  |               |                   |

# CREDIT CARD PAYMENTS

**COMPANY** _____

**AMOUNT OWED** _____

**MINIMUM PAYMENT** _____

**INTEREST RATE** _____

**DUE DATE** _____

| DATE | STARTING BALANCE | PAYMENT VALUE | REMAINING BALANCE |
|------|-----------------|---------------|-------------------|
|      |                 |               |                   |
|      |                 |               |                   |
|      |                 |               |                   |
|      |                 |               |                   |
|      |                 |               |                   |
|      |                 |               |                   |
|      |                 |               |                   |
|      |                 |               |                   |
|      |                 |               |                   |
|      |                 |               |                   |
|      |                 |               |                   |
|      |                 |               |                   |
|      |                 |               |                   |
|      |                 |               |                   |
|      |                 |               |                   |
|      |                 |               |                   |
|      |                 |               |                   |
|      |                 |               |                   |
|      |                 |               |                   |
|      |                 |               |                   |
|      |                 |               |                   |
|      |                 |               |                   |

# CREDIT CARD PAYMENTS

**COMPANY**

**AMOUNT OWED**

**MINIMUM PAYMENT**

**INTEREST RATE**

**DUE DATE**

| DATE | STARTING BALANCE | PAYMENT VALUE | REMAINING BALANCE |
|------|------------------|---------------|-------------------|
|      |                  |               |                   |
|      |                  |               |                   |
|      |                  |               |                   |
|      |                  |               |                   |
|      |                  |               |                   |
|      |                  |               |                   |
|      |                  |               |                   |
|      |                  |               |                   |
|      |                  |               |                   |
|      |                  |               |                   |
|      |                  |               |                   |
|      |                  |               |                   |
|      |                  |               |                   |
|      |                  |               |                   |
|      |                  |               |                   |
|      |                  |               |                   |
|      |                  |               |                   |
|      |                  |               |                   |
|      |                  |               |                   |
|      |                  |               |                   |
|      |                  |               |                   |
|      |                  |               |                   |

# CREDIT CARD PAYMENTS

**COMPANY**

**AMOUNT OWED**

**MINIMUM PAYMENT**

**INTEREST RATE**

**DUE DATE**

| DATE | STARTING BALANCE | PAYMENT VALUE | REMAINING BALANCE |
|------|------------------|---------------|-------------------|
|      |                  |               |                   |
|      |                  |               |                   |
|      |                  |               |                   |
|      |                  |               |                   |
|      |                  |               |                   |
|      |                  |               |                   |
|      |                  |               |                   |
|      |                  |               |                   |
|      |                  |               |                   |
|      |                  |               |                   |
|      |                  |               |                   |
|      |                  |               |                   |
|      |                  |               |                   |
|      |                  |               |                   |
|      |                  |               |                   |
|      |                  |               |                   |
|      |                  |               |                   |
|      |                  |               |                   |
|      |                  |               |                   |
|      |                  |               |                   |
|      |                  |               |                   |
|      |                  |               |                   |

# CREDIT CARD PAYMENTS

**COMPANY**

**AMOUNT OWED**

**MINIMUM PAYMENT**

**INTEREST RATE**

**DUE DATE**

| DATE | STARTING BALANCE | PAYMENT VALUE | REMAINING BALANCE |
|------|------------------|---------------|-------------------|
|      |                  |               |                   |
|      |                  |               |                   |
|      |                  |               |                   |
|      |                  |               |                   |
|      |                  |               |                   |
|      |                  |               |                   |
|      |                  |               |                   |
|      |                  |               |                   |
|      |                  |               |                   |
|      |                  |               |                   |
|      |                  |               |                   |
|      |                  |               |                   |
|      |                  |               |                   |
|      |                  |               |                   |
|      |                  |               |                   |
|      |                  |               |                   |
|      |                  |               |                   |
|      |                  |               |                   |
|      |                  |               |                   |
|      |                  |               |                   |
|      |                  |               |                   |
|      |                  |               |                   |
|      |                  |               |                   |
|      |                  |               |                   |
|      |                  |               |                   |

# CREDIT CARD PAYMENTS

**COMPANY**

**AMOUNT OWED**

**MINIMUM PAYMENT**

**INTEREST RATE**

**DUE DATE**

| DATE | STARTING BALANCE | PAYMENT VALUE | REMAINING BALANCE |
|------|------------------|---------------|-------------------|
|      |                  |               |                   |
|      |                  |               |                   |
|      |                  |               |                   |
|      |                  |               |                   |
|      |                  |               |                   |
|      |                  |               |                   |
|      |                  |               |                   |
|      |                  |               |                   |
|      |                  |               |                   |
|      |                  |               |                   |
|      |                  |               |                   |
|      |                  |               |                   |
|      |                  |               |                   |
|      |                  |               |                   |
|      |                  |               |                   |
|      |                  |               |                   |
|      |                  |               |                   |
|      |                  |               |                   |
|      |                  |               |                   |
|      |                  |               |                   |
|      |                  |               |                   |
|      |                  |               |                   |
|      |                  |               |                   |

# CREDIT CARD PAYMENTS

COMPANY _____

AMOUNT OWED _____

MINIMUM PAYMENT _____

INTEREST RATE _____

DUE DATE _____

| DATE | STARTING BALANCE | PAYMENT VALUE | REMAINING BALANCE |
|------|------------------|---------------|-------------------|
|      |                  |               |                   |
|      |                  |               |                   |
|      |                  |               |                   |
|      |                  |               |                   |
|      |                  |               |                   |
|      |                  |               |                   |
|      |                  |               |                   |
|      |                  |               |                   |
|      |                  |               |                   |
|      |                  |               |                   |
|      |                  |               |                   |
|      |                  |               |                   |
|      |                  |               |                   |
|      |                  |               |                   |
|      |                  |               |                   |
|      |                  |               |                   |
|      |                  |               |                   |
|      |                  |               |                   |
|      |                  |               |                   |
|      |                  |               |                   |
|      |                  |               |                   |
|      |                  |               |                   |

# CREDIT CARD PAYMENTS

**COMPANY**

**AMOUNT OWED**

**MINIMUM PAYMENT**

**INTEREST RATE**

**DUE DATE**

| DATE | STARTING BALANCE | PAYMENT VALUE | REMAINING BALANCE |
|------|------------------|---------------|-------------------|
|      |                  |               |                   |
|      |                  |               |                   |
|      |                  |               |                   |
|      |                  |               |                   |
|      |                  |               |                   |
|      |                  |               |                   |
|      |                  |               |                   |
|      |                  |               |                   |
|      |                  |               |                   |
|      |                  |               |                   |
|      |                  |               |                   |
|      |                  |               |                   |
|      |                  |               |                   |
|      |                  |               |                   |
|      |                  |               |                   |
|      |                  |               |                   |
|      |                  |               |                   |
|      |                  |               |                   |
|      |                  |               |                   |
|      |                  |               |                   |
|      |                  |               |                   |
|      |                  |               |                   |
|      |                  |               |                   |

# CREDIT CARD PAYMENTS

COMPANY

AMOUNT OWED

MINIMUM PAYMENT

INTEREST RATE

DUE DATE

| DATE | STARTING BALANCE | PAYMENT VALUE | REMAINING BALANCE |
|------|------------------|---------------|-------------------|
|      |                  |               |                   |
|      |                  |               |                   |
|      |                  |               |                   |
|      |                  |               |                   |
|      |                  |               |                   |
|      |                  |               |                   |
|      |                  |               |                   |
|      |                  |               |                   |
|      |                  |               |                   |
|      |                  |               |                   |
|      |                  |               |                   |
|      |                  |               |                   |
|      |                  |               |                   |
|      |                  |               |                   |
|      |                  |               |                   |
|      |                  |               |                   |
|      |                  |               |                   |
|      |                  |               |                   |
|      |                  |               |                   |
|      |                  |               |                   |
|      |                  |               |                   |
|      |                  |               |                   |

# CREDIT CARD PAYMENTS

**COMPANY**

**AMOUNT OWED**

**MINIMUM PAYMENT**

**INTEREST RATE**

**DUE DATE**

| DATE | STARTING BALANCE | PAYMENT VALUE | REMAINING BALANCE |
|------|------------------|---------------|-------------------|
|      |                  |               |                   |
|      |                  |               |                   |
|      |                  |               |                   |
|      |                  |               |                   |
|      |                  |               |                   |
|      |                  |               |                   |
|      |                  |               |                   |
|      |                  |               |                   |
|      |                  |               |                   |
|      |                  |               |                   |
|      |                  |               |                   |
|      |                  |               |                   |
|      |                  |               |                   |
|      |                  |               |                   |
|      |                  |               |                   |
|      |                  |               |                   |
|      |                  |               |                   |
|      |                  |               |                   |
|      |                  |               |                   |
|      |                  |               |                   |
|      |                  |               |                   |
|      |                  |               |                   |
|      |                  |               |                   |

# CREDIT CARD PAYMENTS

COMPANY

AMOUNT OWED

MINIMUM PAYMENT

INTEREST RATE

DUE DATE

| DATE | STARTING BALANCE | PAYMENT VALUE | REMAINING BALANCE |
|------|------------------|---------------|-------------------|
|      |                  |               |                   |
|      |                  |               |                   |
|      |                  |               |                   |
|      |                  |               |                   |
|      |                  |               |                   |
|      |                  |               |                   |
|      |                  |               |                   |
|      |                  |               |                   |
|      |                  |               |                   |
|      |                  |               |                   |
|      |                  |               |                   |
|      |                  |               |                   |
|      |                  |               |                   |
|      |                  |               |                   |
|      |                  |               |                   |
|      |                  |               |                   |
|      |                  |               |                   |
|      |                  |               |                   |
|      |                  |               |                   |
|      |                  |               |                   |
|      |                  |               |                   |
|      |                  |               |                   |

# CREDIT CARD PAYMENTS

COMPANY

AMOUNT OWED

MINIMUM PAYMENT

INTEREST RATE

DUE DATE

| DATE | STARTING BALANCE | PAYMENT VALUE | REMAINING BALANCE |
|------|------------------|---------------|-------------------|
|      |                  |               |                   |
|      |                  |               |                   |
|      |                  |               |                   |
|      |                  |               |                   |
|      |                  |               |                   |
|      |                  |               |                   |
|      |                  |               |                   |
|      |                  |               |                   |
|      |                  |               |                   |
|      |                  |               |                   |
|      |                  |               |                   |
|      |                  |               |                   |
|      |                  |               |                   |
|      |                  |               |                   |
|      |                  |               |                   |
|      |                  |               |                   |
|      |                  |               |                   |
|      |                  |               |                   |
|      |                  |               |                   |
|      |                  |               |                   |
|      |                  |               |                   |
|      |                  |               |                   |
|      |                  |               |                   |
|      |                  |               |                   |

# CREDIT CARD PAYMENTS

**COMPANY**

**AMOUNT OWED**

**MINIMUM PAYMENT**

**INTEREST RATE**

**DUE DATE**

| DATE | STARTING BALANCE | PAYMENT VALUE | REMAINING BALANCE |
|------|------------------|---------------|-------------------|
|      |                  |               |                   |
|      |                  |               |                   |
|      |                  |               |                   |
|      |                  |               |                   |
|      |                  |               |                   |
|      |                  |               |                   |
|      |                  |               |                   |
|      |                  |               |                   |
|      |                  |               |                   |
|      |                  |               |                   |
|      |                  |               |                   |
|      |                  |               |                   |
|      |                  |               |                   |
|      |                  |               |                   |
|      |                  |               |                   |
|      |                  |               |                   |
|      |                  |               |                   |
|      |                  |               |                   |
|      |                  |               |                   |
|      |                  |               |                   |
|      |                  |               |                   |
|      |                  |               |                   |
|      |                  |               |                   |

# CREDIT CARD PAYMENTS

**COMPANY**

**AMOUNT OWED**

**MINIMUM PAYMENT**

**INTEREST RATE**

**DUE DATE**

| DATE | STARTING BALANCE | PAYMENT VALUE | REMAINING BALANCE |
|------|------------------|---------------|-------------------|
|      |                  |               |                   |
|      |                  |               |                   |
|      |                  |               |                   |
|      |                  |               |                   |
|      |                  |               |                   |
|      |                  |               |                   |
|      |                  |               |                   |
|      |                  |               |                   |
|      |                  |               |                   |
|      |                  |               |                   |
|      |                  |               |                   |
|      |                  |               |                   |
|      |                  |               |                   |
|      |                  |               |                   |
|      |                  |               |                   |
|      |                  |               |                   |
|      |                  |               |                   |
|      |                  |               |                   |
|      |                  |               |                   |
|      |                  |               |                   |
|      |                  |               |                   |
|      |                  |               |                   |
|      |                  |               |                   |

# CREDIT CARD PAYMENTS

**COMPANY**

**AMOUNT OWED**

**MINIMUM PAYMENT**

**INTEREST RATE**

**DUE DATE**

| DATE | STARTING BALANCE | PAYMENT VALUE | REMAINING BALANCE |
|------|------------------|---------------|-------------------|
|      |                  |               |                   |
|      |                  |               |                   |
|      |                  |               |                   |
|      |                  |               |                   |
|      |                  |               |                   |
|      |                  |               |                   |
|      |                  |               |                   |
|      |                  |               |                   |
|      |                  |               |                   |
|      |                  |               |                   |
|      |                  |               |                   |
|      |                  |               |                   |
|      |                  |               |                   |
|      |                  |               |                   |
|      |                  |               |                   |
|      |                  |               |                   |
|      |                  |               |                   |
|      |                  |               |                   |
|      |                  |               |                   |
|      |                  |               |                   |
|      |                  |               |                   |
|      |                  |               |                   |

# CREDIT CARD PAYMENTS

**COMPANY** _____

**AMOUNT OWED** _____

**MINIMUM PAYMENT** _____

**INTEREST RATE** _____

**DUE DATE** _____

| DATE | STARTING BALANCE | PAYMENT VALUE | REMAINING BALANCE |
|------|------------------|---------------|-------------------|
|      |                  |               |                   |
|      |                  |               |                   |
|      |                  |               |                   |
|      |                  |               |                   |
|      |                  |               |                   |
|      |                  |               |                   |
|      |                  |               |                   |
|      |                  |               |                   |
|      |                  |               |                   |
|      |                  |               |                   |
|      |                  |               |                   |
|      |                  |               |                   |
|      |                  |               |                   |
|      |                  |               |                   |
|      |                  |               |                   |
|      |                  |               |                   |
|      |                  |               |                   |
|      |                  |               |                   |
|      |                  |               |                   |
|      |                  |               |                   |
|      |                  |               |                   |
|      |                  |               |                   |
|      |                  |               |                   |

# CREDIT CARD PAYMENTS

COMPANY

AMOUNT OWED

MINIMUM PAYMENT

INTEREST RATE

DUE DATE

| DATE | STARTING BALANCE | PAYMENT VALUE | REMAINING BALANCE |
|------|------------------|---------------|-------------------|
|      |                  |               |                   |
|      |                  |               |                   |
|      |                  |               |                   |
|      |                  |               |                   |
|      |                  |               |                   |
|      |                  |               |                   |
|      |                  |               |                   |
|      |                  |               |                   |
|      |                  |               |                   |
|      |                  |               |                   |
|      |                  |               |                   |
|      |                  |               |                   |
|      |                  |               |                   |
|      |                  |               |                   |
|      |                  |               |                   |
|      |                  |               |                   |
|      |                  |               |                   |
|      |                  |               |                   |
|      |                  |               |                   |
|      |                  |               |                   |
|      |                  |               |                   |
|      |                  |               |                   |
|      |                  |               |                   |
|      |                  |               |                   |
|      |                  |               |                   |

# CREDIT CARD PAYMENTS

**COMPANY**

**AMOUNT OWED**

**MINIMUM PAYMENT**

**INTEREST RATE**

**DUE DATE**

| DATE | STARTING BALANCE | PAYMENT VALUE | REMAINING BALANCE |
|------|------------------|---------------|-------------------|
|      |                  |               |                   |
|      |                  |               |                   |
|      |                  |               |                   |
|      |                  |               |                   |
|      |                  |               |                   |
|      |                  |               |                   |
|      |                  |               |                   |
|      |                  |               |                   |
|      |                  |               |                   |
|      |                  |               |                   |
|      |                  |               |                   |
|      |                  |               |                   |
|      |                  |               |                   |
|      |                  |               |                   |
|      |                  |               |                   |
|      |                  |               |                   |
|      |                  |               |                   |
|      |                  |               |                   |
|      |                  |               |                   |
|      |                  |               |                   |
|      |                  |               |                   |
|      |                  |               |                   |
|      |                  |               |                   |
|      |                  |               |                   |
|      |                  |               |                   |

# CREDIT CARD PAYMENTS

COMPANY

AMOUNT OWED

MINIMUM PAYMENT

INTEREST RATE

DUE DATE

| DATE | STARTING BALANCE | PAYMENT VALUE | REMAINING BALANCE |
|------|------------------|---------------|-------------------|
|      |                  |               |                   |
|      |                  |               |                   |
|      |                  |               |                   |
|      |                  |               |                   |
|      |                  |               |                   |
|      |                  |               |                   |
|      |                  |               |                   |
|      |                  |               |                   |
|      |                  |               |                   |
|      |                  |               |                   |
|      |                  |               |                   |
|      |                  |               |                   |
|      |                  |               |                   |
|      |                  |               |                   |
|      |                  |               |                   |
|      |                  |               |                   |
|      |                  |               |                   |
|      |                  |               |                   |
|      |                  |               |                   |
|      |                  |               |                   |
|      |                  |               |                   |
|      |                  |               |                   |

# CREDIT CARD PAYMENTS

**COMPANY** _____

**AMOUNT OWED** _____

**MINIMUM PAYMENT** _____

**INTEREST RATE** _____

**DUE DATE** _____

| DATE | STARTING BALANCE | PAYMENT VALUE | REMAINING BALANCE |
|------|------------------|---------------|-------------------|
|      |                  |               |                   |
|      |                  |               |                   |
|      |                  |               |                   |
|      |                  |               |                   |
|      |                  |               |                   |
|      |                  |               |                   |
|      |                  |               |                   |
|      |                  |               |                   |
|      |                  |               |                   |
|      |                  |               |                   |
|      |                  |               |                   |
|      |                  |               |                   |
|      |                  |               |                   |
|      |                  |               |                   |
|      |                  |               |                   |
|      |                  |               |                   |
|      |                  |               |                   |
|      |                  |               |                   |
|      |                  |               |                   |
|      |                  |               |                   |
|      |                  |               |                   |
|      |                  |               |                   |
|      |                  |               |                   |
|      |                  |               |                   |

# CREDIT CARD PAYMENTS

**COMPANY**

**AMOUNT OWED**

**MINIMUM PAYMENT**

**INTEREST RATE**

**DUE DATE**

| DATE | STARTING BALANCE | PAYMENT VALUE | REMAINING BALANCE |
|------|------------------|---------------|-------------------|
|      |                  |               |                   |
|      |                  |               |                   |
|      |                  |               |                   |
|      |                  |               |                   |
|      |                  |               |                   |
|      |                  |               |                   |
|      |                  |               |                   |
|      |                  |               |                   |
|      |                  |               |                   |
|      |                  |               |                   |
|      |                  |               |                   |
|      |                  |               |                   |
|      |                  |               |                   |
|      |                  |               |                   |
|      |                  |               |                   |
|      |                  |               |                   |
|      |                  |               |                   |
|      |                  |               |                   |
|      |                  |               |                   |
|      |                  |               |                   |
|      |                  |               |                   |
|      |                  |               |                   |
|      |                  |               |                   |

# CREDIT CARD PAYMENTS

COMPANY

AMOUNT OWED

MINIMUM PAYMENT

INTEREST RATE

DUE DATE

| DATE | STARTING BALANCE | PAYMENT VALUE | REMAINING BALANCE |
|------|------------------|---------------|-------------------|
|      |                  |               |                   |
|      |                  |               |                   |
|      |                  |               |                   |
|      |                  |               |                   |
|      |                  |               |                   |
|      |                  |               |                   |
|      |                  |               |                   |
|      |                  |               |                   |
|      |                  |               |                   |
|      |                  |               |                   |
|      |                  |               |                   |
|      |                  |               |                   |
|      |                  |               |                   |
|      |                  |               |                   |
|      |                  |               |                   |
|      |                  |               |                   |
|      |                  |               |                   |
|      |                  |               |                   |
|      |                  |               |                   |
|      |                  |               |                   |
|      |                  |               |                   |
|      |                  |               |                   |
|      |                  |               |                   |
|      |                  |               |                   |

# CREDIT CARD PAYMENTS

COMPANY

AMOUNT OWED

MINIMUM PAYMENT

INTEREST RATE

DUE DATE

| DATE | STARTING BALANCE | PAYMENT VALUE | REMAINING BALANCE |
|------|------------------|---------------|-------------------|
|      |                  |               |                   |
|      |                  |               |                   |
|      |                  |               |                   |
|      |                  |               |                   |
|      |                  |               |                   |
|      |                  |               |                   |
|      |                  |               |                   |
|      |                  |               |                   |
|      |                  |               |                   |
|      |                  |               |                   |
|      |                  |               |                   |
|      |                  |               |                   |
|      |                  |               |                   |
|      |                  |               |                   |
|      |                  |               |                   |
|      |                  |               |                   |
|      |                  |               |                   |
|      |                  |               |                   |
|      |                  |               |                   |
|      |                  |               |                   |
|      |                  |               |                   |
|      |                  |               |                   |
|      |                  |               |                   |

# CREDIT CARD PAYMENTS

**COMPANY**

**AMOUNT OWED**

**MINIMUM PAYMENT**

**INTEREST RATE**

**DUE DATE**

| DATE | STARTING BALANCE | PAYMENT VALUE | REMAINING BALANCE |
|------|------------------|---------------|-------------------|
|      |                  |               |                   |
|      |                  |               |                   |
|      |                  |               |                   |
|      |                  |               |                   |
|      |                  |               |                   |
|      |                  |               |                   |
|      |                  |               |                   |
|      |                  |               |                   |
|      |                  |               |                   |
|      |                  |               |                   |
|      |                  |               |                   |
|      |                  |               |                   |
|      |                  |               |                   |
|      |                  |               |                   |
|      |                  |               |                   |
|      |                  |               |                   |
|      |                  |               |                   |
|      |                  |               |                   |
|      |                  |               |                   |
|      |                  |               |                   |
|      |                  |               |                   |
|      |                  |               |                   |
|      |                  |               |                   |
|      |                  |               |                   |

# CREDIT CARD PAYMENTS

COMPANY

AMOUNT OWED

MINIMUM PAYMENT

INTEREST RATE

DUE DATE

| DATE | STARTING BALANCE | PAYMENT VALUE | REMAINING BALANCE |
|------|-----------------|---------------|-------------------|
|      |                 |               |                   |
|      |                 |               |                   |
|      |                 |               |                   |
|      |                 |               |                   |
|      |                 |               |                   |
|      |                 |               |                   |
|      |                 |               |                   |
|      |                 |               |                   |
|      |                 |               |                   |
|      |                 |               |                   |
|      |                 |               |                   |
|      |                 |               |                   |
|      |                 |               |                   |
|      |                 |               |                   |
|      |                 |               |                   |
|      |                 |               |                   |
|      |                 |               |                   |
|      |                 |               |                   |
|      |                 |               |                   |
|      |                 |               |                   |
|      |                 |               |                   |
|      |                 |               |                   |

# CREDIT CARD PAYMENTS

**COMPANY**

**AMOUNT OWED**

**MINIMUM PAYMENT**

**INTEREST RATE**

**DUE DATE**

| DATE | STARTING BALANCE | PAYMENT VALUE | REMAINING BALANCE |
|---|---|---|---|
|  |  |  |  |
|  |  |  |  |
|  |  |  |  |
|  |  |  |  |
|  |  |  |  |
|  |  |  |  |
|  |  |  |  |
|  |  |  |  |
|  |  |  |  |
|  |  |  |  |
|  |  |  |  |
|  |  |  |  |
|  |  |  |  |
|  |  |  |  |
|  |  |  |  |
|  |  |  |  |
|  |  |  |  |
|  |  |  |  |
|  |  |  |  |
|  |  |  |  |
|  |  |  |  |
|  |  |  |  |
|  |  |  |  |
|  |  |  |  |

# CREDIT CARD PAYMENTS

COMPANY

AMOUNT OWED

MINIMUM PAYMENT

INTEREST RATE

DUE DATE

| DATE | STARTING BALANCE | PAYMENT VALUE | REMAINING BALANCE |
|------|------------------|---------------|-------------------|
|      |                  |               |                   |
|      |                  |               |                   |
|      |                  |               |                   |
|      |                  |               |                   |
|      |                  |               |                   |
|      |                  |               |                   |
|      |                  |               |                   |
|      |                  |               |                   |
|      |                  |               |                   |
|      |                  |               |                   |
|      |                  |               |                   |
|      |                  |               |                   |
|      |                  |               |                   |
|      |                  |               |                   |
|      |                  |               |                   |
|      |                  |               |                   |
|      |                  |               |                   |
|      |                  |               |                   |
|      |                  |               |                   |
|      |                  |               |                   |
|      |                  |               |                   |
|      |                  |               |                   |

# CREDIT CARD PAYMENTS

**COMPANY**

**AMOUNT OWED**

**MINIMUM PAYMENT**

**INTEREST RATE**

**DUE DATE**

| DATE | STARTING BALANCE | PAYMENT VALUE | REMAINING BALANCE |
|------|------------------|---------------|-------------------|
|      |                  |               |                   |
|      |                  |               |                   |
|      |                  |               |                   |
|      |                  |               |                   |
|      |                  |               |                   |
|      |                  |               |                   |
|      |                  |               |                   |
|      |                  |               |                   |
|      |                  |               |                   |
|      |                  |               |                   |
|      |                  |               |                   |
|      |                  |               |                   |
|      |                  |               |                   |
|      |                  |               |                   |
|      |                  |               |                   |
|      |                  |               |                   |
|      |                  |               |                   |
|      |                  |               |                   |
|      |                  |               |                   |
|      |                  |               |                   |
|      |                  |               |                   |
|      |                  |               |                   |
|      |                  |               |                   |

# CREDIT CARD PAYMENTS

COMPANY

AMOUNT OWED

MINIMUM PAYMENT

INTEREST RATE

DUE DATE

| DATE | STARTING BALANCE | PAYMENT VALUE | REMAINING BALANCE |
|---|---|---|---|
| | | | |
| | | | |
| | | | |
| | | | |
| | | | |
| | | | |
| | | | |
| | | | |
| | | | |
| | | | |
| | | | |
| | | | |
| | | | |
| | | | |
| | | | |
| | | | |
| | | | |
| | | | |
| | | | |
| | | | |
| | | | |
| | | | |
| | | | |

# CREDIT CARD PAYMENTS

**COMPANY**

**AMOUNT OWED**

**MINIMUM PAYMENT**

**INTEREST RATE**

**DUE DATE**

| DATE | STARTING BALANCE | PAYMENT VALUE | REMAINING BALANCE |
|------|------------------|---------------|-------------------|
|      |                  |               |                   |
|      |                  |               |                   |
|      |                  |               |                   |
|      |                  |               |                   |
|      |                  |               |                   |
|      |                  |               |                   |
|      |                  |               |                   |
|      |                  |               |                   |
|      |                  |               |                   |
|      |                  |               |                   |
|      |                  |               |                   |
|      |                  |               |                   |
|      |                  |               |                   |
|      |                  |               |                   |
|      |                  |               |                   |
|      |                  |               |                   |
|      |                  |               |                   |
|      |                  |               |                   |
|      |                  |               |                   |
|      |                  |               |                   |
|      |                  |               |                   |
|      |                  |               |                   |
|      |                  |               |                   |
|      |                  |               |                   |

# CREDIT CARD PAYMENTS

**COMPANY** _____

**AMOUNT OWED** _____

**MINIMUM PAYMENT** _____

**INTEREST RATE** _____

**DUE DATE** _____

| DATE | STARTING BALANCE | PAYMENT VALUE | REMAINING BALANCE |
|------|------------------|---------------|-------------------|
|      |                  |               |                   |
|      |                  |               |                   |
|      |                  |               |                   |
|      |                  |               |                   |
|      |                  |               |                   |
|      |                  |               |                   |
|      |                  |               |                   |
|      |                  |               |                   |
|      |                  |               |                   |
|      |                  |               |                   |
|      |                  |               |                   |
|      |                  |               |                   |
|      |                  |               |                   |
|      |                  |               |                   |
|      |                  |               |                   |
|      |                  |               |                   |
|      |                  |               |                   |
|      |                  |               |                   |
|      |                  |               |                   |
|      |                  |               |                   |
|      |                  |               |                   |
|      |                  |               |                   |
|      |                  |               |                   |

# CREDIT CARD PAYMENTS

**COMPANY**

**AMOUNT OWED**

**MINIMUM PAYMENT**

**INTEREST RATE**

**DUE DATE**

| DATE | STARTING BALANCE | PAYMENT VALUE | REMAINING BALANCE |
|------|------------------|---------------|-------------------|
|      |                  |               |                   |
|      |                  |               |                   |
|      |                  |               |                   |
|      |                  |               |                   |
|      |                  |               |                   |
|      |                  |               |                   |
|      |                  |               |                   |
|      |                  |               |                   |
|      |                  |               |                   |
|      |                  |               |                   |
|      |                  |               |                   |
|      |                  |               |                   |
|      |                  |               |                   |
|      |                  |               |                   |
|      |                  |               |                   |
|      |                  |               |                   |
|      |                  |               |                   |
|      |                  |               |                   |
|      |                  |               |                   |
|      |                  |               |                   |
|      |                  |               |                   |
|      |                  |               |                   |

# CREDIT CARD PAYMENTS

**COMPANY**

**AMOUNT OWED**

**MINIMUM PAYMENT**

**INTEREST RATE**

**DUE DATE**

| DATE | STARTING BALANCE | PAYMENT VALUE | REMAINING BALANCE |
|------|------------------|---------------|-------------------|
|      |                  |               |                   |
|      |                  |               |                   |
|      |                  |               |                   |
|      |                  |               |                   |
|      |                  |               |                   |
|      |                  |               |                   |
|      |                  |               |                   |
|      |                  |               |                   |
|      |                  |               |                   |
|      |                  |               |                   |
|      |                  |               |                   |
|      |                  |               |                   |
|      |                  |               |                   |
|      |                  |               |                   |
|      |                  |               |                   |
|      |                  |               |                   |
|      |                  |               |                   |
|      |                  |               |                   |
|      |                  |               |                   |
|      |                  |               |                   |
|      |                  |               |                   |
|      |                  |               |                   |

# CREDIT CARD PAYMENTS

COMPANY

AMOUNT OWED

MINIMUM PAYMENT

INTEREST RATE

DUE DATE

| DATE | STARTING BALANCE | PAYMENT VALUE | REMAINING BALANCE |
|---|---|---|---|
|  |  |  |  |
|  |  |  |  |
|  |  |  |  |
|  |  |  |  |
|  |  |  |  |
|  |  |  |  |
|  |  |  |  |
|  |  |  |  |
|  |  |  |  |
|  |  |  |  |
|  |  |  |  |
|  |  |  |  |
|  |  |  |  |
|  |  |  |  |
|  |  |  |  |
|  |  |  |  |
|  |  |  |  |
|  |  |  |  |
|  |  |  |  |
|  |  |  |  |
|  |  |  |  |
|  |  |  |  |

# CREDIT CARD PAYMENTS

COMPANY

AMOUNT OWED

MINIMUM PAYMENT

INTEREST RATE

DUE DATE

| DATE | STARTING BALANCE | PAYMENT VALUE | REMAINING BALANCE |
|------|------------------|---------------|-------------------|
|      |                  |               |                   |
|      |                  |               |                   |
|      |                  |               |                   |
|      |                  |               |                   |
|      |                  |               |                   |
|      |                  |               |                   |
|      |                  |               |                   |
|      |                  |               |                   |
|      |                  |               |                   |
|      |                  |               |                   |
|      |                  |               |                   |
|      |                  |               |                   |
|      |                  |               |                   |
|      |                  |               |                   |
|      |                  |               |                   |
|      |                  |               |                   |
|      |                  |               |                   |
|      |                  |               |                   |
|      |                  |               |                   |
|      |                  |               |                   |
|      |                  |               |                   |
|      |                  |               |                   |
|      |                  |               |                   |

# CREDIT CARD PAYMENTS

**COMPANY**

**AMOUNT OWED**

**MINIMUM PAYMENT**

**INTEREST RATE**

**DUE DATE**

| DATE | STARTING BALANCE | PAYMENT VALUE | REMAINING BALANCE |
|------|------------------|---------------|-------------------|
|      |                  |               |                   |
|      |                  |               |                   |
|      |                  |               |                   |
|      |                  |               |                   |
|      |                  |               |                   |
|      |                  |               |                   |
|      |                  |               |                   |
|      |                  |               |                   |
|      |                  |               |                   |
|      |                  |               |                   |
|      |                  |               |                   |
|      |                  |               |                   |
|      |                  |               |                   |
|      |                  |               |                   |
|      |                  |               |                   |
|      |                  |               |                   |
|      |                  |               |                   |
|      |                  |               |                   |
|      |                  |               |                   |
|      |                  |               |                   |
|      |                  |               |                   |
|      |                  |               |                   |
|      |                  |               |                   |
|      |                  |               |                   |

# CREDIT CARD PAYMENTS

**COMPANY**

**AMOUNT OWED**

**MINIMUM PAYMENT**

**INTEREST RATE**

**DUE DATE**

| DATE | STARTING BALANCE | PAYMENT VALUE | REMAINING BALANCE |
|------|------------------|---------------|-------------------|
|      |                  |               |                   |
|      |                  |               |                   |
|      |                  |               |                   |
|      |                  |               |                   |
|      |                  |               |                   |
|      |                  |               |                   |
|      |                  |               |                   |
|      |                  |               |                   |
|      |                  |               |                   |
|      |                  |               |                   |
|      |                  |               |                   |
|      |                  |               |                   |
|      |                  |               |                   |
|      |                  |               |                   |
|      |                  |               |                   |
|      |                  |               |                   |
|      |                  |               |                   |
|      |                  |               |                   |
|      |                  |               |                   |
|      |                  |               |                   |
|      |                  |               |                   |
|      |                  |               |                   |
|      |                  |               |                   |

# CREDIT CARD PAYMENTS

**COMPANY** _____

**AMOUNT OWED** _____

**MINIMUM PAYMENT** _____

**INTEREST RATE** _____

**DUE DATE** _____

| DATE | STARTING BALANCE | PAYMENT VALUE | REMAINING BALANCE |
|------|------------------|---------------|-------------------|
|      |                  |               |                   |
|      |                  |               |                   |
|      |                  |               |                   |
|      |                  |               |                   |
|      |                  |               |                   |
|      |                  |               |                   |
|      |                  |               |                   |
|      |                  |               |                   |
|      |                  |               |                   |
|      |                  |               |                   |
|      |                  |               |                   |
|      |                  |               |                   |
|      |                  |               |                   |
|      |                  |               |                   |
|      |                  |               |                   |
|      |                  |               |                   |
|      |                  |               |                   |
|      |                  |               |                   |
|      |                  |               |                   |
|      |                  |               |                   |
|      |                  |               |                   |
|      |                  |               |                   |
|      |                  |               |                   |

# CREDIT CARD PAYMENTS

**COMPANY**

**AMOUNT OWED**

**MINIMUM PAYMENT**

**INTEREST RATE**

**DUE DATE**

| DATE | STARTING BALANCE | PAYMENT VALUE | REMAINING BALANCE |
|------|------------------|---------------|-------------------|
|      |                  |               |                   |
|      |                  |               |                   |
|      |                  |               |                   |
|      |                  |               |                   |
|      |                  |               |                   |
|      |                  |               |                   |
|      |                  |               |                   |
|      |                  |               |                   |
|      |                  |               |                   |
|      |                  |               |                   |
|      |                  |               |                   |
|      |                  |               |                   |
|      |                  |               |                   |
|      |                  |               |                   |
|      |                  |               |                   |
|      |                  |               |                   |
|      |                  |               |                   |
|      |                  |               |                   |
|      |                  |               |                   |
|      |                  |               |                   |
|      |                  |               |                   |
|      |                  |               |                   |

# CREDIT CARD PAYMENTS

**COMPANY**

**AMOUNT OWED**

**MINIMUM PAYMENT**

**INTEREST RATE**

**DUE DATE**

| DATE | STARTING BALANCE | PAYMENT VALUE | REMAINING BALANCE |
|------|------------------|---------------|-------------------|
|      |                  |               |                   |
|      |                  |               |                   |
|      |                  |               |                   |
|      |                  |               |                   |
|      |                  |               |                   |
|      |                  |               |                   |
|      |                  |               |                   |
|      |                  |               |                   |
|      |                  |               |                   |
|      |                  |               |                   |
|      |                  |               |                   |
|      |                  |               |                   |
|      |                  |               |                   |
|      |                  |               |                   |
|      |                  |               |                   |
|      |                  |               |                   |
|      |                  |               |                   |
|      |                  |               |                   |
|      |                  |               |                   |
|      |                  |               |                   |
|      |                  |               |                   |
|      |                  |               |                   |
|      |                  |               |                   |
|      |                  |               |                   |

# CREDIT CARD PAYMENTS

COMPANY

AMOUNT OWED

MINIMUM PAYMENT

INTEREST RATE

DUE DATE

| DATE | STARTING BALANCE | PAYMENT VALUE | REMAINING BALANCE |
|------|------------------|---------------|-------------------|
|      |                  |               |                   |
|      |                  |               |                   |
|      |                  |               |                   |
|      |                  |               |                   |
|      |                  |               |                   |
|      |                  |               |                   |
|      |                  |               |                   |
|      |                  |               |                   |
|      |                  |               |                   |
|      |                  |               |                   |
|      |                  |               |                   |
|      |                  |               |                   |
|      |                  |               |                   |
|      |                  |               |                   |
|      |                  |               |                   |
|      |                  |               |                   |
|      |                  |               |                   |
|      |                  |               |                   |
|      |                  |               |                   |
|      |                  |               |                   |
|      |                  |               |                   |
|      |                  |               |                   |
|      |                  |               |                   |
|      |                  |               |                   |
|      |                  |               |                   |
|      |                  |               |                   |

# CREDIT CARD PAYMENTS

COMPANY

AMOUNT OWED

MINIMUM PAYMENT

INTEREST RATE

DUE DATE

| DATE | STARTING BALANCE | PAYMENT VALUE | REMAINING BALANCE |
|------|------------------|---------------|-------------------|
|      |                  |               |                   |
|      |                  |               |                   |
|      |                  |               |                   |
|      |                  |               |                   |
|      |                  |               |                   |
|      |                  |               |                   |
|      |                  |               |                   |
|      |                  |               |                   |
|      |                  |               |                   |
|      |                  |               |                   |
|      |                  |               |                   |
|      |                  |               |                   |
|      |                  |               |                   |
|      |                  |               |                   |
|      |                  |               |                   |
|      |                  |               |                   |
|      |                  |               |                   |
|      |                  |               |                   |
|      |                  |               |                   |
|      |                  |               |                   |
|      |                  |               |                   |
|      |                  |               |                   |
|      |                  |               |                   |
|      |                  |               |                   |
|      |                  |               |                   |

# CREDIT CARD PAYMENTS

**COMPANY**

**AMOUNT OWED**

**MINIMUM PAYMENT**

**INTEREST RATE**

**DUE DATE**

| DATE | STARTING BALANCE | PAYMENT VALUE | REMAINING BALANCE |
|------|------------------|---------------|-------------------|
|      |                  |               |                   |
|      |                  |               |                   |
|      |                  |               |                   |
|      |                  |               |                   |
|      |                  |               |                   |
|      |                  |               |                   |
|      |                  |               |                   |
|      |                  |               |                   |
|      |                  |               |                   |
|      |                  |               |                   |
|      |                  |               |                   |
|      |                  |               |                   |
|      |                  |               |                   |
|      |                  |               |                   |
|      |                  |               |                   |
|      |                  |               |                   |
|      |                  |               |                   |
|      |                  |               |                   |
|      |                  |               |                   |
|      |                  |               |                   |
|      |                  |               |                   |
|      |                  |               |                   |
|      |                  |               |                   |
|      |                  |               |                   |
|      |                  |               |                   |

# CREDIT CARD PAYMENTS

**COMPANY** _____

**AMOUNT OWED** _____

**MINIMUM PAYMENT** _____

**INTEREST RATE** _____

**DUE DATE** _____

| DATE | STARTING BALANCE | PAYMENT VALUE | REMAINING BALANCE |
|------|------------------|---------------|-------------------|
|      |                  |               |                   |
|      |                  |               |                   |
|      |                  |               |                   |
|      |                  |               |                   |
|      |                  |               |                   |
|      |                  |               |                   |
|      |                  |               |                   |
|      |                  |               |                   |
|      |                  |               |                   |
|      |                  |               |                   |
|      |                  |               |                   |
|      |                  |               |                   |
|      |                  |               |                   |
|      |                  |               |                   |
|      |                  |               |                   |
|      |                  |               |                   |
|      |                  |               |                   |
|      |                  |               |                   |
|      |                  |               |                   |
|      |                  |               |                   |
|      |                  |               |                   |
|      |                  |               |                   |
|      |                  |               |                   |
|      |                  |               |                   |

# CREDIT CARD PAYMENTS

COMPANY

AMOUNT OWED

MINIMUM PAYMENT

INTEREST RATE

DUE DATE

| DATE | STARTING BALANCE | PAYMENT VALUE | REMAINING BALANCE |
|------|------------------|---------------|-------------------|
|      |                  |               |                   |
|      |                  |               |                   |
|      |                  |               |                   |
|      |                  |               |                   |
|      |                  |               |                   |
|      |                  |               |                   |
|      |                  |               |                   |
|      |                  |               |                   |
|      |                  |               |                   |
|      |                  |               |                   |
|      |                  |               |                   |
|      |                  |               |                   |
|      |                  |               |                   |
|      |                  |               |                   |
|      |                  |               |                   |
|      |                  |               |                   |
|      |                  |               |                   |
|      |                  |               |                   |
|      |                  |               |                   |
|      |                  |               |                   |
|      |                  |               |                   |
|      |                  |               |                   |
|      |                  |               |                   |
|      |                  |               |                   |
|      |                  |               |                   |

# CREDIT CARD PAYMENTS

COMPANY

AMOUNT OWED

MINIMUM PAYMENT

INTEREST RATE

DUE DATE

| DATE | STARTING BALANCE | PAYMENT VALUE | REMAINING BALANCE |
|------|------------------|---------------|-------------------|
|      |                  |               |                   |
|      |                  |               |                   |
|      |                  |               |                   |
|      |                  |               |                   |
|      |                  |               |                   |
|      |                  |               |                   |
|      |                  |               |                   |
|      |                  |               |                   |
|      |                  |               |                   |
|      |                  |               |                   |
|      |                  |               |                   |
|      |                  |               |                   |
|      |                  |               |                   |
|      |                  |               |                   |
|      |                  |               |                   |
|      |                  |               |                   |
|      |                  |               |                   |
|      |                  |               |                   |
|      |                  |               |                   |
|      |                  |               |                   |
|      |                  |               |                   |
|      |                  |               |                   |
|      |                  |               |                   |
|      |                  |               |                   |
|      |                  |               |                   |

# CREDIT CARD PAYMENTS

COMPANY

AMOUNT OWED

MINIMUM PAYMENT

INTEREST RATE

DUE DATE

| DATE | STARTING BALANCE | PAYMENT VALUE | REMAINING BALANCE |
|------|------------------|---------------|-------------------|
|      |                  |               |                   |
|      |                  |               |                   |
|      |                  |               |                   |
|      |                  |               |                   |
|      |                  |               |                   |
|      |                  |               |                   |
|      |                  |               |                   |
|      |                  |               |                   |
|      |                  |               |                   |
|      |                  |               |                   |
|      |                  |               |                   |
|      |                  |               |                   |
|      |                  |               |                   |
|      |                  |               |                   |
|      |                  |               |                   |
|      |                  |               |                   |
|      |                  |               |                   |
|      |                  |               |                   |
|      |                  |               |                   |
|      |                  |               |                   |
|      |                  |               |                   |
|      |                  |               |                   |
|      |                  |               |                   |
|      |                  |               |                   |

# CREDIT CARD PAYMENTS

COMPANY

AMOUNT OWED

MINIMUM PAYMENT

INTEREST RATE

DUE DATE

| DATE | STARTING BALANCE | PAYMENT VALUE | REMAINING BALANCE |
|------|------------------|---------------|-------------------|
|      |                  |               |                   |
|      |                  |               |                   |
|      |                  |               |                   |
|      |                  |               |                   |
|      |                  |               |                   |
|      |                  |               |                   |
|      |                  |               |                   |
|      |                  |               |                   |
|      |                  |               |                   |
|      |                  |               |                   |
|      |                  |               |                   |
|      |                  |               |                   |
|      |                  |               |                   |
|      |                  |               |                   |
|      |                  |               |                   |
|      |                  |               |                   |
|      |                  |               |                   |
|      |                  |               |                   |
|      |                  |               |                   |
|      |                  |               |                   |
|      |                  |               |                   |
|      |                  |               |                   |
|      |                  |               |                   |
|      |                  |               |                   |
|      |                  |               |                   |

# CREDIT CARD PAYMENTS

**COMPANY**

**AMOUNT OWED**

**MINIMUM PAYMENT**

**INTEREST RATE**

**DUE DATE**

| DATE | STARTING BALANCE | PAYMENT VALUE | REMAINING BALANCE |
|------|------------------|---------------|-------------------|
|      |                  |               |                   |
|      |                  |               |                   |
|      |                  |               |                   |
|      |                  |               |                   |
|      |                  |               |                   |
|      |                  |               |                   |
|      |                  |               |                   |
|      |                  |               |                   |
|      |                  |               |                   |
|      |                  |               |                   |
|      |                  |               |                   |
|      |                  |               |                   |
|      |                  |               |                   |
|      |                  |               |                   |
|      |                  |               |                   |
|      |                  |               |                   |
|      |                  |               |                   |
|      |                  |               |                   |
|      |                  |               |                   |
|      |                  |               |                   |
|      |                  |               |                   |
|      |                  |               |                   |

# CREDIT CARD PAYMENTS

COMPANY

AMOUNT OWED

MINIMUM PAYMENT

INTEREST RATE

DUE DATE

| DATE | STARTING BALANCE | PAYMENT VALUE | REMAINING BALANCE |
|------|------------------|---------------|-------------------|
|      |                  |               |                   |
|      |                  |               |                   |
|      |                  |               |                   |
|      |                  |               |                   |
|      |                  |               |                   |
|      |                  |               |                   |
|      |                  |               |                   |
|      |                  |               |                   |
|      |                  |               |                   |
|      |                  |               |                   |
|      |                  |               |                   |
|      |                  |               |                   |
|      |                  |               |                   |
|      |                  |               |                   |
|      |                  |               |                   |
|      |                  |               |                   |
|      |                  |               |                   |
|      |                  |               |                   |
|      |                  |               |                   |
|      |                  |               |                   |
|      |                  |               |                   |
|      |                  |               |                   |
|      |                  |               |                   |
|      |                  |               |                   |

# CREDIT CARD PAYMENTS

COMPANY

AMOUNT OWED

MINIMUM PAYMENT

INTEREST RATE

DUE DATE

| DATE | STARTING BALANCE | PAYMENT VALUE | REMAINING BALANCE |
|------|-----------------|---------------|-------------------|
|      |                 |               |                   |
|      |                 |               |                   |
|      |                 |               |                   |
|      |                 |               |                   |
|      |                 |               |                   |
|      |                 |               |                   |
|      |                 |               |                   |
|      |                 |               |                   |
|      |                 |               |                   |
|      |                 |               |                   |
|      |                 |               |                   |
|      |                 |               |                   |
|      |                 |               |                   |
|      |                 |               |                   |
|      |                 |               |                   |
|      |                 |               |                   |
|      |                 |               |                   |
|      |                 |               |                   |
|      |                 |               |                   |
|      |                 |               |                   |
|      |                 |               |                   |
|      |                 |               |                   |
|      |                 |               |                   |

# CREDIT CARD PAYMENTS

**COMPANY**

**AMOUNT OWED**

**MINIMUM PAYMENT**

**INTEREST RATE**

**DUE DATE**

| DATE | STARTING BALANCE | PAYMENT VALUE | REMAINING BALANCE |
|------|------------------|---------------|-------------------|
|      |                  |               |                   |
|      |                  |               |                   |
|      |                  |               |                   |
|      |                  |               |                   |
|      |                  |               |                   |
|      |                  |               |                   |
|      |                  |               |                   |
|      |                  |               |                   |
|      |                  |               |                   |
|      |                  |               |                   |
|      |                  |               |                   |
|      |                  |               |                   |
|      |                  |               |                   |
|      |                  |               |                   |
|      |                  |               |                   |
|      |                  |               |                   |
|      |                  |               |                   |
|      |                  |               |                   |
|      |                  |               |                   |
|      |                  |               |                   |
|      |                  |               |                   |
|      |                  |               |                   |
|      |                  |               |                   |

# CREDIT CARD PAYMENTS

**COMPANY**

**AMOUNT OWED**

**MINIMUM PAYMENT**

**INTEREST RATE**

**DUE DATE**

| DATE | STARTING BALANCE | PAYMENT VALUE | REMAINING BALANCE |
|------|------------------|---------------|-------------------|
|      |                  |               |                   |
|      |                  |               |                   |
|      |                  |               |                   |
|      |                  |               |                   |
|      |                  |               |                   |
|      |                  |               |                   |
|      |                  |               |                   |
|      |                  |               |                   |
|      |                  |               |                   |
|      |                  |               |                   |
|      |                  |               |                   |
|      |                  |               |                   |
|      |                  |               |                   |
|      |                  |               |                   |
|      |                  |               |                   |
|      |                  |               |                   |
|      |                  |               |                   |
|      |                  |               |                   |
|      |                  |               |                   |
|      |                  |               |                   |
|      |                  |               |                   |
|      |                  |               |                   |
|      |                  |               |                   |
|      |                  |               |                   |

# CREDIT CARD PAYMENTS

**COMPANY**

**AMOUNT OWED**

**MINIMUM PAYMENT**

**INTEREST RATE**

**DUE DATE**

| DATE | STARTING BALANCE | PAYMENT VALUE | REMAINING BALANCE |
|------|------------------|---------------|-------------------|
|      |                  |               |                   |
|      |                  |               |                   |
|      |                  |               |                   |
|      |                  |               |                   |
|      |                  |               |                   |
|      |                  |               |                   |
|      |                  |               |                   |
|      |                  |               |                   |
|      |                  |               |                   |
|      |                  |               |                   |
|      |                  |               |                   |
|      |                  |               |                   |
|      |                  |               |                   |
|      |                  |               |                   |
|      |                  |               |                   |
|      |                  |               |                   |
|      |                  |               |                   |
|      |                  |               |                   |
|      |                  |               |                   |
|      |                  |               |                   |
|      |                  |               |                   |
|      |                  |               |                   |
|      |                  |               |                   |
|      |                  |               |                   |
|      |                  |               |                   |

# CREDIT CARD PAYMENTS

**COMPANY**

**AMOUNT OWED**

**MINIMUM PAYMENT**

**INTEREST RATE**

**DUE DATE**

| DATE | STARTING BALANCE | PAYMENT VALUE | REMAINING BALANCE |
|------|------------------|---------------|-------------------|
|      |                  |               |                   |
|      |                  |               |                   |
|      |                  |               |                   |
|      |                  |               |                   |
|      |                  |               |                   |
|      |                  |               |                   |
|      |                  |               |                   |
|      |                  |               |                   |
|      |                  |               |                   |
|      |                  |               |                   |
|      |                  |               |                   |
|      |                  |               |                   |
|      |                  |               |                   |
|      |                  |               |                   |
|      |                  |               |                   |
|      |                  |               |                   |
|      |                  |               |                   |
|      |                  |               |                   |
|      |                  |               |                   |
|      |                  |               |                   |
|      |                  |               |                   |
|      |                  |               |                   |

# CREDIT CARD PAYMENTS

**COMPANY**

**AMOUNT OWED**

**MINIMUM PAYMENT**

**INTEREST RATE**

**DUE DATE**

| DATE | STARTING BALANCE | PAYMENT VALUE | REMAINING BALANCE |
|------|------------------|---------------|-------------------|
|      |                  |               |                   |
|      |                  |               |                   |
|      |                  |               |                   |
|      |                  |               |                   |
|      |                  |               |                   |
|      |                  |               |                   |
|      |                  |               |                   |
|      |                  |               |                   |
|      |                  |               |                   |
|      |                  |               |                   |
|      |                  |               |                   |
|      |                  |               |                   |
|      |                  |               |                   |
|      |                  |               |                   |
|      |                  |               |                   |
|      |                  |               |                   |
|      |                  |               |                   |
|      |                  |               |                   |
|      |                  |               |                   |
|      |                  |               |                   |
|      |                  |               |                   |
|      |                  |               |                   |
|      |                  |               |                   |

# CREDIT CARD PAYMENTS

**COMPANY**

**AMOUNT OWED**

**MINIMUM PAYMENT**

**INTEREST RATE**

**DUE DATE**

| DATE | STARTING BALANCE | PAYMENT VALUE | REMAINING BALANCE |
|------|------------------|---------------|-------------------|
|      |                  |               |                   |
|      |                  |               |                   |
|      |                  |               |                   |
|      |                  |               |                   |
|      |                  |               |                   |
|      |                  |               |                   |
|      |                  |               |                   |
|      |                  |               |                   |
|      |                  |               |                   |
|      |                  |               |                   |
|      |                  |               |                   |
|      |                  |               |                   |
|      |                  |               |                   |
|      |                  |               |                   |
|      |                  |               |                   |
|      |                  |               |                   |
|      |                  |               |                   |
|      |                  |               |                   |
|      |                  |               |                   |
|      |                  |               |                   |
|      |                  |               |                   |
|      |                  |               |                   |

# CREDIT CARD PAYMENTS

COMPANY

AMOUNT OWED

MINIMUM PAYMENT

INTEREST RATE

DUE DATE

| DATE | STARTING BALANCE | PAYMENT VALUE | REMAINING BALANCE |
|------|------------------|---------------|-------------------|
|      |                  |               |                   |
|      |                  |               |                   |
|      |                  |               |                   |
|      |                  |               |                   |
|      |                  |               |                   |
|      |                  |               |                   |
|      |                  |               |                   |
|      |                  |               |                   |
|      |                  |               |                   |
|      |                  |               |                   |
|      |                  |               |                   |
|      |                  |               |                   |
|      |                  |               |                   |
|      |                  |               |                   |
|      |                  |               |                   |
|      |                  |               |                   |
|      |                  |               |                   |
|      |                  |               |                   |
|      |                  |               |                   |
|      |                  |               |                   |
|      |                  |               |                   |
|      |                  |               |                   |
|      |                  |               |                   |
|      |                  |               |                   |

# CREDIT CARD PAYMENTS

**COMPANY** _____

**AMOUNT OWED** _____

**MINIMUM PAYMENT** _____

**INTEREST RATE** _____

**DUE DATE** _____

| DATE | STARTING BALANCE | PAYMENT VALUE | REMAINING BALANCE |
|------|------------------|---------------|-------------------|
|      |                  |               |                   |
|      |                  |               |                   |
|      |                  |               |                   |
|      |                  |               |                   |
|      |                  |               |                   |
|      |                  |               |                   |
|      |                  |               |                   |
|      |                  |               |                   |
|      |                  |               |                   |
|      |                  |               |                   |
|      |                  |               |                   |
|      |                  |               |                   |
|      |                  |               |                   |
|      |                  |               |                   |
|      |                  |               |                   |
|      |                  |               |                   |
|      |                  |               |                   |
|      |                  |               |                   |
|      |                  |               |                   |
|      |                  |               |                   |
|      |                  |               |                   |
|      |                  |               |                   |
|      |                  |               |                   |

# CREDIT CARD PAYMENTS

COMPANY

AMOUNT OWED

MINIMUM PAYMENT

INTEREST RATE

DUE DATE

| DATE | STARTING BALANCE | PAYMENT VALUE | REMAINING BALANCE |
|------|------------------|---------------|-------------------|
|      |                  |               |                   |
|      |                  |               |                   |
|      |                  |               |                   |
|      |                  |               |                   |
|      |                  |               |                   |
|      |                  |               |                   |
|      |                  |               |                   |
|      |                  |               |                   |
|      |                  |               |                   |
|      |                  |               |                   |
|      |                  |               |                   |
|      |                  |               |                   |
|      |                  |               |                   |
|      |                  |               |                   |
|      |                  |               |                   |
|      |                  |               |                   |
|      |                  |               |                   |
|      |                  |               |                   |
|      |                  |               |                   |
|      |                  |               |                   |
|      |                  |               |                   |
|      |                  |               |                   |
|      |                  |               |                   |
|      |                  |               |                   |

# CREDIT CARD PAYMENTS

**COMPANY**

**AMOUNT OWED**

**MINIMUM PAYMENT**

**INTEREST RATE**

**DUE DATE**

| DATE | STARTING BALANCE | PAYMENT VALUE | REMAINING BALANCE |
|------|------------------|---------------|-------------------|
|      |                  |               |                   |
|      |                  |               |                   |
|      |                  |               |                   |
|      |                  |               |                   |
|      |                  |               |                   |
|      |                  |               |                   |
|      |                  |               |                   |
|      |                  |               |                   |
|      |                  |               |                   |
|      |                  |               |                   |
|      |                  |               |                   |
|      |                  |               |                   |
|      |                  |               |                   |
|      |                  |               |                   |
|      |                  |               |                   |
|      |                  |               |                   |
|      |                  |               |                   |
|      |                  |               |                   |
|      |                  |               |                   |
|      |                  |               |                   |
|      |                  |               |                   |
|      |                  |               |                   |
|      |                  |               |                   |

# CREDIT CARD PAYMENTS

**COMPANY**

**AMOUNT OWED**

**MINIMUM PAYMENT**

**INTEREST RATE**

**DUE DATE**

| DATE | STARTING BALANCE | PAYMENT VALUE | REMAINING BALANCE |
|------|------------------|---------------|-------------------|
|      |                  |               |                   |
|      |                  |               |                   |
|      |                  |               |                   |
|      |                  |               |                   |
|      |                  |               |                   |
|      |                  |               |                   |
|      |                  |               |                   |
|      |                  |               |                   |
|      |                  |               |                   |
|      |                  |               |                   |
|      |                  |               |                   |
|      |                  |               |                   |
|      |                  |               |                   |
|      |                  |               |                   |
|      |                  |               |                   |
|      |                  |               |                   |
|      |                  |               |                   |
|      |                  |               |                   |
|      |                  |               |                   |
|      |                  |               |                   |
|      |                  |               |                   |
|      |                  |               |                   |
|      |                  |               |                   |

# CREDIT CARD PAYMENTS

COMPANY

AMOUNT OWED

MINIMUM PAYMENT

INTEREST RATE

DUE DATE

| DATE | STARTING BALANCE | PAYMENT VALUE | REMAINING BALANCE |
|------|------------------|---------------|-------------------|
|      |                  |               |                   |
|      |                  |               |                   |
|      |                  |               |                   |
|      |                  |               |                   |
|      |                  |               |                   |
|      |                  |               |                   |
|      |                  |               |                   |
|      |                  |               |                   |
|      |                  |               |                   |
|      |                  |               |                   |
|      |                  |               |                   |
|      |                  |               |                   |
|      |                  |               |                   |
|      |                  |               |                   |
|      |                  |               |                   |
|      |                  |               |                   |
|      |                  |               |                   |
|      |                  |               |                   |
|      |                  |               |                   |
|      |                  |               |                   |
|      |                  |               |                   |
|      |                  |               |                   |
|      |                  |               |                   |

# CREDIT CARD PAYMENTS

**COMPANY**

**AMOUNT OWED**

**MINIMUM PAYMENT**

**INTEREST RATE**

**DUE DATE**

| DATE | STARTING BALANCE | PAYMENT VALUE | REMAINING BALANCE |
|------|------------------|---------------|-------------------|
|      |                  |               |                   |
|      |                  |               |                   |
|      |                  |               |                   |
|      |                  |               |                   |
|      |                  |               |                   |
|      |                  |               |                   |
|      |                  |               |                   |
|      |                  |               |                   |
|      |                  |               |                   |
|      |                  |               |                   |
|      |                  |               |                   |
|      |                  |               |                   |
|      |                  |               |                   |
|      |                  |               |                   |
|      |                  |               |                   |
|      |                  |               |                   |
|      |                  |               |                   |
|      |                  |               |                   |
|      |                  |               |                   |
|      |                  |               |                   |
|      |                  |               |                   |
|      |                  |               |                   |
|      |                  |               |                   |

# CREDIT CARD PAYMENTS

**COMPANY**

**AMOUNT OWED**

**MINIMUM PAYMENT**

**INTEREST RATE**

**DUE DATE**

| DATE | STARTING BALANCE | PAYMENT VALUE | REMAINING BALANCE |
|------|------------------|---------------|-------------------|
|      |                  |               |                   |
|      |                  |               |                   |
|      |                  |               |                   |
|      |                  |               |                   |
|      |                  |               |                   |
|      |                  |               |                   |
|      |                  |               |                   |
|      |                  |               |                   |
|      |                  |               |                   |
|      |                  |               |                   |
|      |                  |               |                   |
|      |                  |               |                   |
|      |                  |               |                   |
|      |                  |               |                   |
|      |                  |               |                   |
|      |                  |               |                   |
|      |                  |               |                   |
|      |                  |               |                   |
|      |                  |               |                   |
|      |                  |               |                   |
|      |                  |               |                   |
|      |                  |               |                   |
|      |                  |               |                   |
|      |                  |               |                   |

# CREDIT CARD PAYMENTS

COMPANY

AMOUNT OWED

MINIMUM PAYMENT

INTEREST RATE

DUE DATE

| DATE | STARTING BALANCE | PAYMENT VALUE | REMAINING BALANCE |
|------|------------------|---------------|-------------------|
|      |                  |               |                   |
|      |                  |               |                   |
|      |                  |               |                   |
|      |                  |               |                   |
|      |                  |               |                   |
|      |                  |               |                   |
|      |                  |               |                   |
|      |                  |               |                   |
|      |                  |               |                   |
|      |                  |               |                   |
|      |                  |               |                   |
|      |                  |               |                   |
|      |                  |               |                   |
|      |                  |               |                   |
|      |                  |               |                   |
|      |                  |               |                   |
|      |                  |               |                   |
|      |                  |               |                   |
|      |                  |               |                   |
|      |                  |               |                   |
|      |                  |               |                   |
|      |                  |               |                   |
|      |                  |               |                   |
|      |                  |               |                   |
|      |                  |               |                   |

# CREDIT CARD PAYMENTS

COMPANY

AMOUNT OWED

MINIMUM PAYMENT

INTEREST RATE

DUE DATE

| DATE | STARTING BALANCE | PAYMENT VALUE | REMAINING BALANCE |
|------|------------------|---------------|-------------------|
|      |                  |               |                   |
|      |                  |               |                   |
|      |                  |               |                   |
|      |                  |               |                   |
|      |                  |               |                   |
|      |                  |               |                   |
|      |                  |               |                   |
|      |                  |               |                   |
|      |                  |               |                   |
|      |                  |               |                   |
|      |                  |               |                   |
|      |                  |               |                   |
|      |                  |               |                   |
|      |                  |               |                   |
|      |                  |               |                   |
|      |                  |               |                   |
|      |                  |               |                   |
|      |                  |               |                   |
|      |                  |               |                   |
|      |                  |               |                   |
|      |                  |               |                   |
|      |                  |               |                   |

# CREDIT CARD PAYMENTS

**COMPANY** _____

**AMOUNT OWED** _____

**MINIMUM PAYMENT** _____

**INTEREST RATE** _____

**DUE DATE** _____

| DATE | STARTING BALANCE | PAYMENT VALUE | REMAINING BALANCE |
|------|------------------|---------------|-------------------|
|      |                  |               |                   |
|      |                  |               |                   |
|      |                  |               |                   |
|      |                  |               |                   |
|      |                  |               |                   |
|      |                  |               |                   |
|      |                  |               |                   |
|      |                  |               |                   |
|      |                  |               |                   |
|      |                  |               |                   |
|      |                  |               |                   |
|      |                  |               |                   |
|      |                  |               |                   |
|      |                  |               |                   |
|      |                  |               |                   |
|      |                  |               |                   |
|      |                  |               |                   |
|      |                  |               |                   |
|      |                  |               |                   |
|      |                  |               |                   |
|      |                  |               |                   |
|      |                  |               |                   |
|      |                  |               |                   |

# CREDIT CARD PAYMENTS

COMPANY

AMOUNT OWED

MINIMUM PAYMENT

INTEREST RATE

DUE DATE

| DATE | STARTING BALANCE | PAYMENT VALUE | REMAINING BALANCE |
|------|------------------|---------------|-------------------|
|      |                  |               |                   |
|      |                  |               |                   |
|      |                  |               |                   |
|      |                  |               |                   |
|      |                  |               |                   |
|      |                  |               |                   |
|      |                  |               |                   |
|      |                  |               |                   |
|      |                  |               |                   |
|      |                  |               |                   |
|      |                  |               |                   |
|      |                  |               |                   |
|      |                  |               |                   |
|      |                  |               |                   |
|      |                  |               |                   |
|      |                  |               |                   |
|      |                  |               |                   |
|      |                  |               |                   |
|      |                  |               |                   |
|      |                  |               |                   |
|      |                  |               |                   |
|      |                  |               |                   |
|      |                  |               |                   |

# CREDIT CARD PAYMENTS

**COMPANY**

**AMOUNT OWED**

**MINIMUM PAYMENT**

**INTEREST RATE**

**DUE DATE**

| DATE | STARTING BALANCE | PAYMENT VALUE | REMAINING BALANCE |
|------|------------------|---------------|-------------------|
|      |                  |               |                   |
|      |                  |               |                   |
|      |                  |               |                   |
|      |                  |               |                   |
|      |                  |               |                   |
|      |                  |               |                   |
|      |                  |               |                   |
|      |                  |               |                   |
|      |                  |               |                   |
|      |                  |               |                   |
|      |                  |               |                   |
|      |                  |               |                   |
|      |                  |               |                   |
|      |                  |               |                   |
|      |                  |               |                   |
|      |                  |               |                   |
|      |                  |               |                   |
|      |                  |               |                   |
|      |                  |               |                   |
|      |                  |               |                   |
|      |                  |               |                   |
|      |                  |               |                   |
|      |                  |               |                   |

# CREDIT CARD PAYMENTS

COMPANY

AMOUNT OWED

MINIMUM PAYMENT

INTEREST RATE

DUE DATE

| DATE | STARTING BALANCE | PAYMENT VALUE | REMAINING BALANCE |
|---|---|---|---|
|  |  |  |  |
|  |  |  |  |
|  |  |  |  |
|  |  |  |  |
|  |  |  |  |
|  |  |  |  |
|  |  |  |  |
|  |  |  |  |
|  |  |  |  |
|  |  |  |  |
|  |  |  |  |
|  |  |  |  |
|  |  |  |  |
|  |  |  |  |
|  |  |  |  |
|  |  |  |  |
|  |  |  |  |
|  |  |  |  |
|  |  |  |  |
|  |  |  |  |
|  |  |  |  |
|  |  |  |  |
|  |  |  |  |
|  |  |  |  |

# CREDIT CARD PAYMENTS

**COMPANY**

**AMOUNT OWED**

**MINIMUM PAYMENT**

**INTEREST RATE**

**DUE DATE**

| DATE | STARTING BALANCE | PAYMENT VALUE | REMAINING BALANCE |
|---|---|---|---|
| | | | |
| | | | |
| | | | |
| | | | |
| | | | |
| | | | |
| | | | |
| | | | |
| | | | |
| | | | |
| | | | |
| | | | |
| | | | |
| | | | |
| | | | |
| | | | |
| | | | |
| | | | |
| | | | |
| | | | |
| | | | |
| | | | |
| | | | |
| | | | |

# CREDIT CARD PAYMENTS

**COMPANY** _____

**AMOUNT OWED** _____

**MINIMUM PAYMENT** _____

**INTEREST RATE** _____

**DUE DATE** _____

| DATE | STARTING BALANCE | PAYMENT VALUE | REMAINING BALANCE |
|------|------------------|---------------|-------------------|
|      |                  |               |                   |
|      |                  |               |                   |
|      |                  |               |                   |
|      |                  |               |                   |
|      |                  |               |                   |
|      |                  |               |                   |
|      |                  |               |                   |
|      |                  |               |                   |
|      |                  |               |                   |
|      |                  |               |                   |
|      |                  |               |                   |
|      |                  |               |                   |
|      |                  |               |                   |
|      |                  |               |                   |
|      |                  |               |                   |
|      |                  |               |                   |
|      |                  |               |                   |
|      |                  |               |                   |
|      |                  |               |                   |
|      |                  |               |                   |
|      |                  |               |                   |
|      |                  |               |                   |
|      |                  |               |                   |

# CREDIT CARD PAYMENTS

**COMPANY** _____

**AMOUNT OWED** _____

**MINIMUM PAYMENT** _____

**INTEREST RATE** _____

**DUE DATE** _____

| DATE | STARTING BALANCE | PAYMENT VALUE | REMAINING BALANCE |
|------|------------------|---------------|-------------------|
|      |                  |               |                   |
|      |                  |               |                   |
|      |                  |               |                   |
|      |                  |               |                   |
|      |                  |               |                   |
|      |                  |               |                   |
|      |                  |               |                   |
|      |                  |               |                   |
|      |                  |               |                   |
|      |                  |               |                   |
|      |                  |               |                   |
|      |                  |               |                   |
|      |                  |               |                   |
|      |                  |               |                   |
|      |                  |               |                   |
|      |                  |               |                   |
|      |                  |               |                   |
|      |                  |               |                   |
|      |                  |               |                   |
|      |                  |               |                   |
|      |                  |               |                   |
|      |                  |               |                   |
|      |                  |               |                   |

# CREDIT CARD PAYMENTS

COMPANY

AMOUNT OWED

MINIMUM PAYMENT

INTEREST RATE

DUE DATE

| DATE | STARTING BALANCE | PAYMENT VALUE | REMAINING BALANCE |
|------|------------------|---------------|-------------------|
|      |                  |               |                   |
|      |                  |               |                   |
|      |                  |               |                   |
|      |                  |               |                   |
|      |                  |               |                   |
|      |                  |               |                   |
|      |                  |               |                   |
|      |                  |               |                   |
|      |                  |               |                   |
|      |                  |               |                   |
|      |                  |               |                   |
|      |                  |               |                   |
|      |                  |               |                   |
|      |                  |               |                   |
|      |                  |               |                   |
|      |                  |               |                   |
|      |                  |               |                   |
|      |                  |               |                   |
|      |                  |               |                   |
|      |                  |               |                   |
|      |                  |               |                   |
|      |                  |               |                   |
|      |                  |               |                   |

# CREDIT CARD PAYMENTS

**COMPANY**

**AMOUNT OWED**

**MINIMUM PAYMENT**

**INTEREST RATE**

**DUE DATE**

| DATE | STARTING BALANCE | PAYMENT VALUE | REMAINING BALANCE |
|------|------------------|---------------|-------------------|
|      |                  |               |                   |
|      |                  |               |                   |
|      |                  |               |                   |
|      |                  |               |                   |
|      |                  |               |                   |
|      |                  |               |                   |
|      |                  |               |                   |
|      |                  |               |                   |
|      |                  |               |                   |
|      |                  |               |                   |
|      |                  |               |                   |
|      |                  |               |                   |
|      |                  |               |                   |
|      |                  |               |                   |
|      |                  |               |                   |
|      |                  |               |                   |
|      |                  |               |                   |
|      |                  |               |                   |
|      |                  |               |                   |
|      |                  |               |                   |
|      |                  |               |                   |
|      |                  |               |                   |
|      |                  |               |                   |
|      |                  |               |                   |

# CREDIT CARD PAYMENTS

**COMPANY**

**AMOUNT OWED**

**MINIMUM PAYMENT**

**INTEREST RATE**

**DUE DATE**

| DATE | STARTING BALANCE | PAYMENT VALUE | REMAINING BALANCE |
|------|------------------|---------------|-------------------|
|      |                  |               |                   |
|      |                  |               |                   |
|      |                  |               |                   |
|      |                  |               |                   |
|      |                  |               |                   |
|      |                  |               |                   |
|      |                  |               |                   |
|      |                  |               |                   |
|      |                  |               |                   |
|      |                  |               |                   |
|      |                  |               |                   |
|      |                  |               |                   |
|      |                  |               |                   |
|      |                  |               |                   |
|      |                  |               |                   |
|      |                  |               |                   |
|      |                  |               |                   |
|      |                  |               |                   |
|      |                  |               |                   |
|      |                  |               |                   |
|      |                  |               |                   |
|      |                  |               |                   |
|      |                  |               |                   |

# CREDIT CARD PAYMENTS

**COMPANY**

**AMOUNT OWED**

**MINIMUM PAYMENT**

**INTEREST RATE**

**DUE DATE**

| DATE | STARTING BALANCE | PAYMENT VALUE | REMAINING BALANCE |
|------|------------------|---------------|-------------------|
|      |                  |               |                   |
|      |                  |               |                   |
|      |                  |               |                   |
|      |                  |               |                   |
|      |                  |               |                   |
|      |                  |               |                   |
|      |                  |               |                   |
|      |                  |               |                   |
|      |                  |               |                   |
|      |                  |               |                   |
|      |                  |               |                   |
|      |                  |               |                   |
|      |                  |               |                   |
|      |                  |               |                   |
|      |                  |               |                   |
|      |                  |               |                   |
|      |                  |               |                   |
|      |                  |               |                   |
|      |                  |               |                   |
|      |                  |               |                   |
|      |                  |               |                   |
|      |                  |               |                   |
|      |                  |               |                   |
|      |                  |               |                   |
|      |                  |               |                   |

# CREDIT CARD PAYMENTS

**COMPANY**

**AMOUNT OWED**

**MINIMUM PAYMENT**

**INTEREST RATE**

**DUE DATE**

| DATE | STARTING BALANCE | PAYMENT VALUE | REMAINING BALANCE |
|---|---|---|---|
| | | | |
| | | | |
| | | | |
| | | | |
| | | | |
| | | | |
| | | | |
| | | | |
| | | | |
| | | | |
| | | | |
| | | | |
| | | | |
| | | | |
| | | | |
| | | | |
| | | | |
| | | | |
| | | | |
| | | | |
| | | | |
| | | | |
| | | | |

# CREDIT CARD PAYMENTS

**COMPANY**

**AMOUNT OWED**

**MINIMUM PAYMENT**

**INTEREST RATE**

**DUE DATE**

| DATE | STARTING BALANCE | PAYMENT VALUE | REMAINING BALANCE |
|------|------------------|---------------|-------------------|
|      |                  |               |                   |
|      |                  |               |                   |
|      |                  |               |                   |
|      |                  |               |                   |
|      |                  |               |                   |
|      |                  |               |                   |
|      |                  |               |                   |
|      |                  |               |                   |
|      |                  |               |                   |
|      |                  |               |                   |
|      |                  |               |                   |
|      |                  |               |                   |
|      |                  |               |                   |
|      |                  |               |                   |
|      |                  |               |                   |
|      |                  |               |                   |
|      |                  |               |                   |
|      |                  |               |                   |
|      |                  |               |                   |
|      |                  |               |                   |
|      |                  |               |                   |
|      |                  |               |                   |

# CREDIT CARD PAYMENTS

COMPANY

AMOUNT OWED

MINIMUM PAYMENT

INTEREST RATE

DUE DATE

| DATE | STARTING BALANCE | PAYMENT VALUE | REMAINING BALANCE |
|---|---|---|---|
| | | | |
| | | | |
| | | | |
| | | | |
| | | | |
| | | | |
| | | | |
| | | | |
| | | | |
| | | | |
| | | | |
| | | | |
| | | | |
| | | | |
| | | | |
| | | | |
| | | | |
| | | | |
| | | | |
| | | | |
| | | | |
| | | | |

# CREDIT CARD PAYMENTS

**COMPANY**

**AMOUNT OWED**

**MINIMUM PAYMENT**

**INTEREST RATE**

**DUE DATE**

| DATE | STARTING BALANCE | PAYMENT VALUE | REMAINING BALANCE |
|------|------------------|---------------|-------------------|
|      |                  |               |                   |
|      |                  |               |                   |
|      |                  |               |                   |
|      |                  |               |                   |
|      |                  |               |                   |
|      |                  |               |                   |
|      |                  |               |                   |
|      |                  |               |                   |
|      |                  |               |                   |
|      |                  |               |                   |
|      |                  |               |                   |
|      |                  |               |                   |
|      |                  |               |                   |
|      |                  |               |                   |
|      |                  |               |                   |
|      |                  |               |                   |
|      |                  |               |                   |
|      |                  |               |                   |
|      |                  |               |                   |
|      |                  |               |                   |
|      |                  |               |                   |
|      |                  |               |                   |

# CREDIT CARD PAYMENTS

**COMPANY**

**AMOUNT OWED**

**MINIMUM PAYMENT**

**INTEREST RATE**

**DUE DATE**

| DATE | STARTING BALANCE | PAYMENT VALUE | REMAINING BALANCE |
|------|------------------|---------------|-------------------|
|      |                  |               |                   |
|      |                  |               |                   |
|      |                  |               |                   |
|      |                  |               |                   |
|      |                  |               |                   |
|      |                  |               |                   |
|      |                  |               |                   |
|      |                  |               |                   |
|      |                  |               |                   |
|      |                  |               |                   |
|      |                  |               |                   |
|      |                  |               |                   |
|      |                  |               |                   |
|      |                  |               |                   |
|      |                  |               |                   |
|      |                  |               |                   |
|      |                  |               |                   |
|      |                  |               |                   |
|      |                  |               |                   |
|      |                  |               |                   |
|      |                  |               |                   |
|      |                  |               |                   |

# CREDIT CARD PAYMENTS

COMPANY

AMOUNT OWED

MINIMUM PAYMENT

INTEREST RATE

DUE DATE

| DATE | STARTING BALANCE | PAYMENT VALUE | REMAINING BALANCE |
|------|------------------|---------------|-------------------|
|      |                  |               |                   |
|      |                  |               |                   |
|      |                  |               |                   |
|      |                  |               |                   |
|      |                  |               |                   |
|      |                  |               |                   |
|      |                  |               |                   |
|      |                  |               |                   |
|      |                  |               |                   |
|      |                  |               |                   |
|      |                  |               |                   |
|      |                  |               |                   |
|      |                  |               |                   |
|      |                  |               |                   |
|      |                  |               |                   |
|      |                  |               |                   |
|      |                  |               |                   |
|      |                  |               |                   |
|      |                  |               |                   |
|      |                  |               |                   |
|      |                  |               |                   |
|      |                  |               |                   |
|      |                  |               |                   |

# CREDIT CARD PAYMENTS

**COMPANY**

**AMOUNT OWED**

**MINIMUM PAYMENT**

**INTEREST RATE**

**DUE DATE**

| DATE | STARTING BALANCE | PAYMENT VALUE | REMAINING BALANCE |
|------|------------------|---------------|-------------------|
|      |                  |               |                   |
|      |                  |               |                   |
|      |                  |               |                   |
|      |                  |               |                   |
|      |                  |               |                   |
|      |                  |               |                   |
|      |                  |               |                   |
|      |                  |               |                   |
|      |                  |               |                   |
|      |                  |               |                   |
|      |                  |               |                   |
|      |                  |               |                   |
|      |                  |               |                   |
|      |                  |               |                   |
|      |                  |               |                   |
|      |                  |               |                   |
|      |                  |               |                   |
|      |                  |               |                   |
|      |                  |               |                   |
|      |                  |               |                   |
|      |                  |               |                   |
|      |                  |               |                   |
|      |                  |               |                   |

# CREDIT CARD PAYMENTS

**COMPANY**

**AMOUNT OWED**

**MINIMUM PAYMENT**

**INTEREST RATE**

**DUE DATE**

| DATE | STARTING BALANCE | PAYMENT VALUE | REMAINING BALANCE |
|------|------------------|---------------|-------------------|
|      |                  |               |                   |
|      |                  |               |                   |
|      |                  |               |                   |
|      |                  |               |                   |
|      |                  |               |                   |
|      |                  |               |                   |
|      |                  |               |                   |
|      |                  |               |                   |
|      |                  |               |                   |
|      |                  |               |                   |
|      |                  |               |                   |
|      |                  |               |                   |
|      |                  |               |                   |
|      |                  |               |                   |
|      |                  |               |                   |
|      |                  |               |                   |
|      |                  |               |                   |
|      |                  |               |                   |
|      |                  |               |                   |
|      |                  |               |                   |
|      |                  |               |                   |
|      |                  |               |                   |

# CREDIT CARD PAYMENTS

COMPANY

AMOUNT OWED

MINIMUM PAYMENT

INTEREST RATE

DUE DATE

| DATE | STARTING BALANCE | PAYMENT VALUE | REMAINING BALANCE |
|------|------------------|---------------|-------------------|
|      |                  |               |                   |
|      |                  |               |                   |
|      |                  |               |                   |
|      |                  |               |                   |
|      |                  |               |                   |
|      |                  |               |                   |
|      |                  |               |                   |
|      |                  |               |                   |
|      |                  |               |                   |
|      |                  |               |                   |
|      |                  |               |                   |
|      |                  |               |                   |
|      |                  |               |                   |
|      |                  |               |                   |
|      |                  |               |                   |
|      |                  |               |                   |
|      |                  |               |                   |
|      |                  |               |                   |
|      |                  |               |                   |
|      |                  |               |                   |
|      |                  |               |                   |
|      |                  |               |                   |
|      |                  |               |                   |

# CREDIT CARD PAYMENTS

COMPANY

AMOUNT OWED

MINIMUM PAYMENT

INTEREST RATE

DUE DATE

| DATE | STARTING BALANCE | PAYMENT VALUE | REMAINING BALANCE |
|------|------------------|---------------|-------------------|
|      |                  |               |                   |
|      |                  |               |                   |
|      |                  |               |                   |
|      |                  |               |                   |
|      |                  |               |                   |
|      |                  |               |                   |
|      |                  |               |                   |
|      |                  |               |                   |
|      |                  |               |                   |
|      |                  |               |                   |
|      |                  |               |                   |
|      |                  |               |                   |
|      |                  |               |                   |
|      |                  |               |                   |
|      |                  |               |                   |
|      |                  |               |                   |
|      |                  |               |                   |
|      |                  |               |                   |
|      |                  |               |                   |
|      |                  |               |                   |
|      |                  |               |                   |
|      |                  |               |                   |

# CREDIT CARD PAYMENTS

COMPANY

AMOUNT OWED

MINIMUM PAYMENT

INTEREST RATE

DUE DATE

| DATE | STARTING BALANCE | PAYMENT VALUE | REMAINING BALANCE |
|------|------------------|---------------|-------------------|
|      |                  |               |                   |
|      |                  |               |                   |
|      |                  |               |                   |
|      |                  |               |                   |
|      |                  |               |                   |
|      |                  |               |                   |
|      |                  |               |                   |
|      |                  |               |                   |
|      |                  |               |                   |
|      |                  |               |                   |
|      |                  |               |                   |
|      |                  |               |                   |
|      |                  |               |                   |
|      |                  |               |                   |
|      |                  |               |                   |
|      |                  |               |                   |
|      |                  |               |                   |
|      |                  |               |                   |
|      |                  |               |                   |
|      |                  |               |                   |
|      |                  |               |                   |
|      |                  |               |                   |
|      |                  |               |                   |

# CREDIT CARD PAYMENTS

**COMPANY**

**AMOUNT OWED**

**MINIMUM PAYMENT**

**INTEREST RATE**

**DUE DATE**

| DATE | STARTING BALANCE | PAYMENT VALUE | REMAINING BALANCE |
|------|------------------|---------------|-------------------|
|      |                  |               |                   |
|      |                  |               |                   |
|      |                  |               |                   |
|      |                  |               |                   |
|      |                  |               |                   |
|      |                  |               |                   |
|      |                  |               |                   |
|      |                  |               |                   |
|      |                  |               |                   |
|      |                  |               |                   |
|      |                  |               |                   |
|      |                  |               |                   |
|      |                  |               |                   |
|      |                  |               |                   |
|      |                  |               |                   |
|      |                  |               |                   |
|      |                  |               |                   |
|      |                  |               |                   |
|      |                  |               |                   |
|      |                  |               |                   |
|      |                  |               |                   |
|      |                  |               |                   |
|      |                  |               |                   |
|      |                  |               |                   |

# CREDIT CARD PAYMENTS

COMPANY

AMOUNT OWED

MINIMUM PAYMENT

INTEREST RATE

DUE DATE

| DATE | STARTING BALANCE | PAYMENT VALUE | REMAINING BALANCE |
|---|---|---|---|
| | | | |
| | | | |
| | | | |
| | | | |
| | | | |
| | | | |
| | | | |
| | | | |
| | | | |
| | | | |
| | | | |
| | | | |
| | | | |
| | | | |
| | | | |
| | | | |
| | | | |
| | | | |
| | | | |
| | | | |
| | | | |
| | | | |

# CREDIT CARD PAYMENTS

**COMPANY**

**AMOUNT OWED**

**MINIMUM PAYMENT**

**INTEREST RATE**

**DUE DATE**

| DATE | STARTING BALANCE | PAYMENT VALUE | REMAINING BALANCE |
|------|------------------|---------------|-------------------|
|      |                  |               |                   |
|      |                  |               |                   |
|      |                  |               |                   |
|      |                  |               |                   |
|      |                  |               |                   |
|      |                  |               |                   |
|      |                  |               |                   |
|      |                  |               |                   |
|      |                  |               |                   |
|      |                  |               |                   |
|      |                  |               |                   |
|      |                  |               |                   |
|      |                  |               |                   |
|      |                  |               |                   |
|      |                  |               |                   |
|      |                  |               |                   |
|      |                  |               |                   |
|      |                  |               |                   |
|      |                  |               |                   |
|      |                  |               |                   |
|      |                  |               |                   |
|      |                  |               |                   |
|      |                  |               |                   |

www.ingramcontent.com/pod-product-compliance
Lightning Source LLC
Chambersburg PA
CBHW051033030426
42336CB00015B/2850